# MANIC.

ALSO BY ANGELA SOLIS

WHAT LIES IN THE WOLF'S HEART

# MANIC.

A COLLECTION OF POETRY

BY

ANGELA SOLIS

NOT ONLY SO, BUT WE ALSO
GLORY IN OUR SUFFERINGS,
BECAUSE WE KNOW THAT
SUFFERING PRODUCES
P E R S E V E R A N C E;
PERSEVERANCE, CHARACTER;
AND CHARACTER, HOPE.

ROMANS 5:3-4

# DEDICATION

PADRE Y MADRE

You taught me at an early age that if I have something to say, then it should be expressed, even if people didn't agree with it, or if it got me into trouble because then it meant that I'm using my voice. Thank you for encouraging me to use it, I wouldn't be the unapologetic outspoken filter-less smartass woman that I am today without you two. You raised me the best you could with what you had & I promise that I will spend the rest of my life trying to be even half of the beautiful souls you two are & keep making you proud.


JESSICA G.

Since the beginning, 2012, you've been there & I intend to have you here till the end, & just thank you from the bottom of my heart for sticking with me & believing in me since day one that I will one day reach the level of self-love that I deserve towards myself. 8 years later & I finally reached it Jess, we did it, thank you for being patient & seeing it, seeing me, before I ever could.


ASHLEY F.

To my military sister a.k.a NorCal girl, who got this whole book situation started, thank you for challenging me & knowing that I can always rise to it, to past relationship decisions, life decisions, & down to these books. Thank you for helping me open this chapter of my life, so with that, here's to the second one, Ash.

MCKENNAH N.

I've said it before, and I will say it again, you were divine timing within my life. We grew – and still are – growing in so many aspects of life together. You've inspired me to chase after the self-love that I have been missing, you helped guide me to my Faith in a way I never thought I could have & always desired. Thank you for being so selfless & always wanting to push me to be a better me. You're one of the gems that I never thought I would be lucky enough to have.

MARISOL N.

You were taken too early, but I know God always has a reason, & He didn't want you to suffer anymore. I wish you could read the words that I have for you but I know you're here over my shoulder & in my heart as my guardian angel. Thank you for being the woman who saw a 16 year old girl & loved her unconditionally like her own daughter as well as her family & loved them like her own. You're forever missed & endlessly loved mom.

## ACKNWOLEDGEMENTS

RACHEL S.

VICTORIA S.

JOSEPHINE A.

JESSICA G.

ASHLEY F.

MCKENNAH N.

RACHEL C.

ALYCIA R.

# FOREWORD

by R. Clift

*As I sit here, piecing together the finishing touches of the design of this heartfelt manuscript— I am filled with the charged energy of the challenge to write only a few words on this author.*

*As a poet, I often find myself surrounded by voices. It can be difficult to distinguish one from the other— but ever since the very first time I read Angela's poetry— on some warm August day in 2019— her voice has always come through as resolutely singular.*

*We began as strangers on that August day, distanced by the void of online communication, but in time we would grow not only to be working together regularly, but to be close friends. It is not oftentimes that one, from so very far away, will have the ability to understand you on a selfless, soul-level, but for Angela— this is something that she does naturally.*

*You will read of her intense desire for true connection in these poems, you will read of her triumphs, truths, and darkest moments. What you are holding in your hands is more than a book of rhythmic words, this is a piece of a woman's soul. This is courage in physical form.*

*From working with Angela on her first book "What Lies in the Wolf's Heart" to watching this book go from just an idea to a full-steam-ahead passion project— I have seen growth within a human being more apparent than anyone else in my life. To witness a person, a friend, grow into themselves— challenge themselves— strive for healing and strive for life, has been more of a privilege than I could ever express.*

I have always believed that poetry, more than anything, is a journey of self discovery. A diving inwards, a chance to uncover parts of oneself that will widen and enrich that inner place in which we must always reside.

Within these pages, you are allowed to be a passenger to Angela's own inner journey. You have the rare opportunity to see inside a poet's heart, mind, and soul as they spend months braving depths, processing the past, living boldly in the present, and making vows for the future.

"To be an artist is to look at a tragedy and innately see the beauty in it." I wrote those words in June of 2019 as I was traveling through Greece— I believe they reached across oceans to find who they truly belonged to.

As I wrote them, I didn't really know who I was writing them for or about— maybe everyone, maybe no one— but now, I am sure.

That artist is the woman who would come into my life only a month later. That artist is the woman who has fully embraced poetry as a central part of her being. That artist is Angela Solis, who's eyes may be the most difficult to read that I have ever known, but I can say, with certainty, that they innately see beauty in the tragedies of this world. Maybe, that's all that matters.

May you find a quiet place to let these words soak into your bones, may your mind and soul be transported by her narrative, and may you close this book with the understanding that you are not alone.

- R. Clift, author of *To Feel Anything at All*,
*To Be Remembered, Until We Meet Again,*
*Your Thoughts Deserve a Decent Place to Live*

Tennessee, January, 2021

"Have patience with everything that remains unsolved in your heart. Try to love the questions themselves, like locked rooms and like books written in a foreign language.

Do not now look for the answers. They cannot now be given to you because you could not live them. It is a question of experiencing everything. At present you need to live the question.

Perhaps you will gradually, without even noticing it, find yourself experiencing the answer, some distant day."

*- Rainer Maria Rilke, Letters to a Young Poet*

# CONTENTS

# I : GENESIS

If I'm being honest,
A huge reason why I decided
to publish
my first book, and now my second,
is because if my demons
ever take full control of my conscious,
and I successfully give up,
I'd at least have some
form of me left in existence
for you to grasp
in your hands.

# MANIC.

I'll start off this poem
by stating that I'm not going to lie and say
I understand what you're going through,
because I don't.
Your internal battle is just as unique and different
as every individuals' own fingerprint.
I'm not going to feed you lies
and tell you everything will be alright
because at the moment,
I know you're not fine,
and if I'm being honest,
neither am I.
I'm a bit too stubborn
and I'm not very open
about my own problems, or mental health
unless it brings some sort of substance,
so, in this instance,
I hope it helps.
I understand keeping quiet
about your emotions
because you don't want to be a burden
from expressing the honest feelings
and thoughts from your head,
but if I'm going to give you any advice,
I'd say to open up and try.
Ask for help, please.
I've tried to kill myself twice,

and I'm not proud to say it out loud
or read it from a paper sheet being typed,
but it's the truth
and it's something I can't hide.
So, I'm here to tell you,
you really aren't alone.
Even if we can't physically be in reach,
there's texting, calling, and endless resources
with today's technology.
Just please, please be strong for yourself.
I know it's not easy, but just keep fighting.
So, the next time your weight gets too heavy,
here's the hotline,
1-800-273-8255.

# MANIC.

I'm feeling too much again,
I'm getting too empathetic,
and I think it has
to deal with the fact
that I can't ease her pain
as much as I would like to.
I want to take all of it.
I would trade places
with her in an instant
even if it meant everything
would be given to me.

Tell me that I can help her
in some way, shape or form
besides just physically being here
because I'm torn.
Tell me I can help heal her more,
please.
All I keep seeing
is her unresolved demons jumping
around in her eyes
that are just attacking her mind
as if it's some sort of game.

She's in arms reach
right across from me
with the coffee table being
the only thing separating us.
She's surrounded with love, poetry
and me
as she has a genuine happy smile,
but, all I want to say to her is,
*sweetie, everything will be alright.*
Yet, at the same time,
I feel like I would be speaking a lie
because I can't take anything away
from what happened in Hawaii.

But, at least
what I do know
is that I can do my best to try
and be any puzzle piece
that she needs
to help her in her healing journey
because nothing would ever be
too mentally demanding
for me if that means she gets to heal properly.

# MANIC.

A suicidal mind is fragile
no matter how hardened
o n e s   e x t e r i o r
may look or how bright
their smile may be.

ANGELA SOLIS

I

A

M

F

R

A

G

I

L

E

# MANIC.

How ironic
it is
to see the rolled white stick
filled with nicotine
between your lips.

As I've seen
y o u r   b u r n s
from the cigarette tip
on your right rib,
chest, and pelvis.

Ultimately leaving prominent scars
on your skin.

I've been resorting
to needle therapy
quite a bit recently in an
attempt to feel something.

Thankfully,

it has been working
because the needle tip
is turning my bleeding skin
on my ribs to art
as opposed to scars.

# MANIC.

I have so much love
to offer you from my cup
but it seems like you have no clue
what to do
with any of it
because all you do is dilute
every ounce that I give you.

I don't know why I put effort
toward stitching
a heart that's still beating.

The sutures
tear out from the pressure
of wanting to remain open
despite the constant infections
entering the wound.

Maybe I'm attracted
to the feeling,
maybe I'm addicted
to the healing.

# MANIC.

I'VE EXHAUSTED SO MUCH ENERGY
INTO YOUR HEALTH INSTEAD OF MINE,
AND I THINK THAT'S WHERE THE WHOLE PROBLEM LIED.

IT WAS NEVER HEALTHY.

Your apologies
are all over due,
they're just left-over residue
from your tongue
that can't seem to get enough
of giving meaningless
words and excuses to try and justify
w h y  t h e y  n e v e r  m a t c h
your actions.

# MANIC.

I remember when I was practically
forced again into therapy,
it wasn't the best feeling
to say the least.
I've already been through this back in middle school.
I just sat down at a table
with a lady across from me
who was gripping a brown clipboard
while asking me questions
that I refused to answer
because to me,
my problems and actions
was none of their business,
so, I would automatically become defensive.
But this time around, I admit,
it was a little different.
I was in a position
where I had to make effort in my progress,
I had to be open to possibly
being prescribed medication
even though I was adamant
and utterly against it
since the very beginning.

But, if I didn't show any positive progression
in our meetings,
or complete the homework assignments
that she sent me home with,
I would be obligated
to take more sessions
at my therapist's discretion.
So, that's exactly what happened,
I had to see her three times a week
with an occasional checkup call every
Monday morning
after every weekend
to account for my presence
and make sure that I didn't successfully commit
since I was on the high priority list.
Every week I would check in,
fill out a questionnaire on the laptop,
or paper sheet
depending on if the computers weren't working,
and sit at the same chair in the back corner
closest to her door
waiting for her to call me into her office
to pick up where we left off
from the previous session.

# MANIC.

We talked about more than I ever expected
because I eventually
became so comfortable
that I finally admitted when I had first attempted,
as well as the second,
as she told me,
"If you would have told me about this
when it first happened,
you would have been admitted,
no doubt about it."
But the thing is,
I already knew that.
I thought about the consequences
and the time period
between the attempts and when I'd confess
to avoid repercussions
because I didn't want to become an inpatient
and have my freedom taken.
So, I had to be patient
and choose my time to be honest
about everything wisely,
and I couldn't stand it.
I had so many voices running
through my head
that I already didn't know how to deal with,
and were hard enough to control all alone.
So, in my defense,
I didn't want to be punished
for my decisions,
I just wanted to get it all off of my chest.

The weeks passed by
and we continued doing more exercises
as well as officially setting
a meeting up with a psychiatrist
that prescribed me medication
no matter how much I couldn't stand it.
But I had to make it look
like I was cooperating
in that aspect,
so, I would pick up my meds prescribed by Dr. S
from the pharmacy window
and I would come home
and throw the pills out of my view.
I never took one, I refused.
We constantly
talked about things
over and over and over again,
she told me it was called *exposure therapy.*
I felt as if I wasn't making any progress
and would continuously be questioning
the point of all of this,
it was so overwhelming.
She kept dissecting
my past traumas
that I never wanted to bring back up
and unraveling every tangled string
with ease
with her charts and specific questions.
All of my problems would lead
back to one person, and if it didn't,
then the problem was me,
at least that's what I would see.

# MANIC.

But, she would constantly reassure
me and tell me that it wasn't
and my feelings were relevant.
Or that it was okay to have anger
towards the events that I was put through
and experienced when I was younger
and to understand that my fear of abandonment
was not a feeling of exaggeration.
But for whatever reason,
I couldn't be.

She knew that I never wanted to talk about her
because I didn't want to put any negative
images or energy to her name.
What about her perspective on everything?
What about her story?
Lord knows she never had the opportunity
to express her feelings
in a healthy way
or receive the proper treatment like me
and be able to afford therapy.
I have too much empathy,
I keep thinking about her problems
that never received any guidance or clarity.
She was going through difficult things.
A divorce, a disconnected relationship
between her own mother and daughter,
struggling to put food on the table for her kids
because she was jobless.

Constantly wondering
when the child support was coming in
and how she'd pay rent on time
with the constant fear of eviction
at the back of her head.
She was just overwhelmed and stressed,
and at one point, she was dying
because of the radiation treatment
from being diagnosed with cancer,
and not just once, but twice.

So, looking back at everything
and taking in every piece
of advice from therapy
that helped me mend my broken pieces
that I never knew existed
and affected my relationships,
I can still never be angry,
but only forgiving and love her wholeheartedly
for giving me everything
when we had nothing.
That's the true healing

— FORGIVING.

FOR SOMEONE WHO TALKS A LOT
ABOUT ATTACHMENT,

IT'S PRETTY IRONIC
TO SIMULTANEOUSLY
NOT WANT IT.

Take off those
rose gold lenses
for just a second.
I think your glasses
are becoming an obstruction
to your vision
because they're clouding your judgement
and making you oblivious
to what's toxic.
I know you don't want to acknowledge
all the flag's that are red
and admit
that you've been avoiding this topic
because you're so invested,
but, no relationship
is worth it
if you're losing yourself
in the process.

# MANIC.

My voice was trembling
uncontrollably
as I sent you a seven minute
and twenty-three second
audio message
of me explaining my perspective
to you of why I need you to respect
my distance
and boundaries that I'm setting
in order to preserve my energy
because I need this separation for healing
to truly manifest
in my well being
rather than being invested
in your problems and situations.

I stand by my decision
of creating this separation
because you've admitted
to feeling the emptiness

caused by my absence
ever since I stopped checking in
since I was the only one who ever did,
and I can't seem to wrap my head
around the whole concept
of you taking my effort and communication
for granted
without having to ask myself
if you ever even valued my presence
when you actually had it
in the first place,
but I guess not,
because if you truly appreciated it,
you wouldn't have put yourself in a position
for it to be lost,
but it's no longer part of my problem
because you no longer have access.

# MANIC.

All I ever wanted
was to be enough.
To be tucked
in your pocket of love
and fit like a glove,
but,
you pushed me under the rug
with the rest of the dust
and poured salt on
every one of my cuts,
leaving me with only
broken trust.

HOW MUCH MORE OF YOU
AND YOUR DEAD WEIGHT
DO I HAVE TO CARRY
IN ORDER FOR YOU TO REALIZE THAT MY
KNEES
WILL EVENTUALLY
BUCKLE FROM BEING
SO FATIGUED?

# MANIC.

"I fucking hate
that I won't hear from you,
I got so used to
you checking in
on me or talking to me
that the absence of you in my daily
life took a great toll on me.
I'm sorry.
I took that communication for granted."

I'm sorry for you, too,
because I don't think
we can go back
to
how
we
used
to
be.

I've had ink
coursing and running
through my veins all day.

And yet,
I still couldn't find a way
to articulate
it out onto a page.

Your colors
have been losing all of its exposure
and saturation.

Who's been draining
your palette
and violating your utensil tips?

You've been negligent towards your motions
and careless of your grip,
causing your illustrations
to become mixed
and uneven.

But, I guess
I should have anticipated this
and lowered my expectations
of you as an Artist
because you eventually became
a  h a b i t  o f  d e s t r u c t i o n
towards your own blends.

# MANIC.

If you asked me which tattoo
of mine
was my favorite,
I wouldn't be able to decide,
how could I ever pick?
I love every single one.
So, why would I ever think
of doing a cover up
just because we're no longer
involved in each other's lives?

*Should I just get this*
*tattoo covered up?*
*I guess that's my last question.*

Why would you ask me this?
That's your decision
to make, and only yours.

Are my words on your skin
no longer important
or bring any more significance?
Because when I said:

*"I have to admit,*
*that I couldn't help resist*
*to give the compliment*
*to someone so angelic*

*because as soon as the clouds*
*began to shift,*
*and the colors began to eclipse,*
*everything else became oblivious*
*as soon as I saw your radiance..."*
I meant every bit of punctuation.

Are you ashamed of our commitment
from when we mutually decided
to get matching Roman bible versus
that literally voices,
*"...We also glory in our sufferings,*
*because we know that suffering*
*produces perseverance..."*
Are those words no longer relevant?

I'm not sure what your answer concluded,
because I never responded
with my opinion,
but all I know is,
whatever you pick,
I respect and support it,
because just like every poem previously
dedicated to you,
this one is too.

# MANIC.

I'm no longer codependent
on your presence,
or temporary attention
that would always
determine my emotions.

I tethered towards your validation
in the little compliments.
I refused to bring attention
towards certain topics
even when they disturbed my conscious
because I wanted to avoid confrontation;
the problem was never valid.
I constantly fell back into regression,
which I now know stemmed
from childhood neglect
because I refused to address
or pay any acknowledgment
towards my own self abandonment.
I figured I wasn't important
enough and would be irrelevant.

So, you see,
I was attentive
towards my habits and choices,
but only to a certain extent.

I chose against having such clarity
and decided to keep my vision blurry
and remain in ignorant bliss
because I wanted to fix
your situations,
even though I was cognizant
enough to know that I couldn't.

I can't mend everything
especially when I'm not the one who needs fixing.

YOUR PERMANENT INK
SPREAD ALL OVER MY DELICATE SHEETS
AND RIPPED THEM AWAY CARELESSLY
BECAUSE YOUR HANDS
WERE TOO HEAVY
AND UNSTEADY.

# MANIC.

Your tongue is tainted
with lies,
and I don't understand why
I choose to listen.

Your hands are saturated
with lust
and false promises
as if you could ever hold yourself
to such decisions.
But, I let your grip
s i n k   i n t o   m e   a n y w a y.

I just can't resist
the seductive portion
of your dialect
even when I know that there's no benefit.

But, here I am again,
getting sucked right back in
when I know I shouldn't.

— I can never learn my lesson.

I held my breath
with you, time and time again.
Every thought, or opinion,
I had to second guess
if they were even worth a mention,
and if not, they became suppressed.

I never wanted to argue,
or have any kind of dispute
because I knew
you would never be able to see my point of you.
So, overtime,
I learned to become mute.

I held my breath,
and because of this,
I lost sight of my own conscience
since I was only invested
in your words
that inevitably made me suffocate
from being trapped around my chest
as tightly as a corset.

# MANIC.

Is missing you
part of your prescription description?
Because I'm having signs and symptoms
of a mental health relapse
and I don't know where to start at
besides resorting back
to memories of what we had.

Hearing your voice became a craving
to the point
that I'd start to hear your melodies
in the words you'd speak
as I'd play videos of us on repeat
just to hear the way you used to talk to me.

Or, I'd often catch myself fixating
on becoming intertwined and glued
to you
while caressing
every part of your frame in a sensual interlude.

I'm not sure what to do in order to suppress
all the thoughts of you in my head,
or how to alleviate the weight
of you off my chest.
But, I think I can start with
putting an end to the trend
of losing myself in the process
of loving you
and gaining enough self-respect
by finally putting myself first,
and you second.

I'm usually one to follow my intuition
but, in this instance,
I second guessed it
because I thought you were different.

I just wish
I would have been able to predict
that our relationship
would have ended up like this,
because all I know is
you were worth it,
so, I gave you every inch
of me without hesitation
because to me,
you deserved it.

# MANIC.

I understand.

Trust me,
you feeling the need
like you have to do any type of explaining
about why you don't trust easily
is the last thing
that you will ever have to do
w i t h   m e.

I understand, baby.

I know a thing or two
about being told everything under the sun
and then some
which caused walls to build up,
or being pushed to the point
of becoming defensive
because of an abundant
amount of previous experiences
that inevitably became redundant
due to me having a high tolerance
of patience.

I understand.

The mournful process
of becoming lost within your own self refection
and carrying the feeling of neglect
when you mention
the topic of emptiness and lack of fulfillment
due to a lack of reciprocation
because of their words never matching their actions
and pinky promises
developing the habit
of becoming  B  R  O  K  E  N.

You're not alone in this,
I understand all of it,
and that's what's unfortunate.

ANSWER MY QUESTION.
HOW AM I SUPPOSED TO MENTION
ANY TYPE OF FUTURE WITHOUT YOU IN IT
WHEN YOU'RE ALL I'VE EVER ENVISIONED?

# MANIC.

I still can't pin point the moment
that I got lost in your translation
because I can no longer understand
your language.

I'm in need of a linguist
to help interpret
your message.

But, the thing is,
I'm hesitant
to know if I even want to read it.

I thought of you,
but that's nothing new.

I looked for you
in things I never used to.

I just want to make the attempt
to text or call
and make sure that you're healthy and staying safe
considering that we are in a pandemic,
but, it'll just mitigate my progress.

I just can't help it,
but, regardless of the temptation,
I  r e s i s t
because I know that that's what's best.
I'm the one who had to leave anyway,
despite how much I was invested
and wanted to stay.
So, what kind of sense would it make
to turn back to someone
when I'm the one who walked away.

# MANIC.

We just left the bar
and now you're in my face
calling me insulting names
while constantly
emphasizing that you mean every word,
as you block me from going into the truck
since you want to finish up
what you have to say,
as if I couldn't tell deep down that you're hurt.

"If you were a guy, I'd fuck you up,
I'd choke the fuck out of you,
you're a stupid bitch and a cunt."

All I kept responding
with was "thank you"
or nodding my head with acknowledgment
towards your thoughts and opinions
of me
because honestly
you're just temporary and not worth my energy,
and I also didn't know what else to say.
I don't want to entertain
your rage and anger,
because I know men like you feed off of it.
You feed off of control
and dominance.
Just answer my question,
a r e   y o u   d o n e   y e t ?
Oh, nope, there's more
you're not finished.

"Also, you're not as pretty
as you think you are.
You need to check your shit
and get yourself together
because you ain't shit"

Tell me, man
where else are you trying to hit me at
that I already haven't told myself
time and time again?
You're just another voice in my head,
and the only difference
is that the voice is now from your perspective.
I hope you were able to let
everything off of your chest
and had a good night's rest,
because I did.

MANIC.

YOU

WERE

THE

ADRENALINE

f
l
o
w
i
n
g

THROUGH ME

FOR
SO
LONG,
THAT EVENTUALLY YOU
BECAME AN ADDICTION
THROUGHOUT MY BEING.

YOU'D FLOW WITHIN MY BODY
FILLING MY VEINS AND ARTERIES
CLOGGING MY BLOODSTREAM.

AND IF I DIDN'T HAVE YOU IN MY HANDS,
I WOULD RELAPSE,
BECAUSE I DIDN'T KNOW
HOW TO HANDLE
YOUR
ABSENCE.

# MANIC.

I'm usually not one to do this,
but, now that I think about it,
I should have taken a minute
and eased my way in.

I thought I'd be fine,
but that was a lie
because then I realized
that I could no longer accept
you in miniature pieces,
since I had you exclusively.

I've become impatient

because now I know what it's like
to be full
off of you
since I've consumed
too much of you.

I UNDERSTAND TOO, YOU KNOW,
WHAT IF FEELS LIKE TO REJECT
CERTAIN GESTURES
AND HAVING DIFFICULTY ACCEPTING
GOOD THINGS
BECAUSE YOU FEEL AS IF YOU'RE UNDESERVING.

POETRY IS UP FOR INTERPRETATION.
I CAN'T FORCE MY MESSAGE
INTO THE WORDS THAT I INTENDED
INTO YOUR SIGHT OF VISION.

*"I'm not gonna fight*
*for someone who wants to cut ties."*

That's rich of you say,
where were you that night?
W h e r e   w a s   y o u r   l o y a l t y
when somebody who is inevitably
going to become temporary
started to threaten to lay hands on me
in front of you?

There wasn't an ounce
of fighting for me then,
why are you making it sound like it's irrelevant
to now take action?
You might as well have left
me without water
in a drought,
because that's what it felt like.

So, don't tell me that I'm not worth fighting for
when you failed to before.

## MANIC.

I'm usually
not the type to worry,
or be hesitant and cautious
with my own actions and decisions.
But, in this instance,
there's an exception.

I'm mentally available,
and that's what makes me vulnerable.

I'm vulnerable to you,
and I'm not sure what to do.

I'm stuck between
respecting what we have because it's what I value
and wanting to confess and pursue
my feelings,
or leaving them out in limbo
out of fear of it being a one-sided thing.

YOU LEFT ME CONGESTED
FROM HOLDING
ONTO SO MANY EMOTIONS,
I DON'T KNOW WHERE TO DROP THEM.
MY BRAIN IS BECOMING SWOLLEN
AND OVERCROWDED.

THERE'S ONLY SO MUCH POETRY I CAN
PUT IN MOTION
BEFORE I LOSE MY ESSENCE
IN THE MANIC.

# MANIC.

I personally
don't think you'd be able to comprehend
the thoughts I have towards my own self
in my conscience.

They de-rail me quite often
from being so negative.

The moment
that I believe I'm making some sort of progress
is the second
that I fall back into my toxic habit
that I've grown
so comfortable to know.

Why do I hold
onto something that hinders my growth?
How do you escape a prison
when you're the one
who locked yourself in?
How do you leave a cage
when it's your own headspace?

I couldn't give you an exact answer
to my questions
even if that's what I wanted,
but, I hope you can relate.

It sucks doesn't it?
The moment that everything goes sour
the instant
that you decide to let your guard down.

They don't value you anymore
like they said they supposedly did.
It makes you second guess
if they ever meant such a thing before.

They're willing to let you go
at the drop of a dime,
while holding open the door.

# MANIC.

WHEN I THINK ABOUT IT, IT'S TRAGIC
HOW MUCH MANIPULATION
I TOLERATED,
EVEN MY PARENTS NOTICED.

SO, IF YOU WANT TO KNOW THE SECRET
BEHIND THE DISASTER WITHIN OUR RECIPE,
YOU WERE THE MAIN INGREDIENT
WITHOUT QUESTION.

I haven't written poetry in a week,
maybe
it's because nothing is coming to me.
Or maybe
there's an underlying condition
that I'm avoiding
because the moment it gets addressed
is the instant I'll have to confront it.

# MANIC.

If I actually confess and decide to be honest,
then I'll admit
that I've subconsciously left
copious amounts of suicide notes
in the form of voicemails and messages.

I never asked for this,
why would I ever want it?
There's been so many instances
where my depression
has caused me to self-inflict
because it manipulated me
by making me believe
that harming myself was the only option.

I never wanted my wrists red,
but it's kind of difficult to avoid temptation
when you left my message on read
when I needed your help to get out of my own head.

Mental illness,
it has a mind of its own,
you become forced to sit
within your own affliction,
it's unpredictable and chaotic.
You can never guess the type of mindset
you'll be put in,
or how much endorphins and serotonin
will become suppressed
in a matter of minutes
because of the chemical imbalance.

But all I know is,
no matter how difficult this battle has been,
I'm going to win.

HOW MANY METAPHORS
AND MESSAGES
DO I HAVE TO COME UP WITH BEFORE
YOU CAN FINALLY REALIZE
AND GET IT THROUGH YOUR HEAD
THAT I'M NO LONGER
GOING TO REMAIN A VICTIM OF YOUR GRIP?

# MANIC.

I DON'T UNDERSTAND THIS GENERATION.

EVERYONE WANTS TO RUN FROM CONNECTION
AS IF IT'S SOME SORT OF SIN.

If I gave you my love
would you keep it?
If I opened up,
would you have honest intentions
and not take advantage?
If I gave you all of me
would it be reciprocated?

I don't want to be hurt again.

# MANIC.

*I love you.*

...

*I love you more.*

I'm chucking uncontrollably,
oh, sweetie,
no, you don't.
We've been through this,
every time I'd ask you the questions,
"Do you? How do you love me more?"
And put you in the spotlight,
you'd remain quiet
and choose to change the topic.
I'm constantly left guessing
on where I stand
with you when I know I shouldn't.

You'd tell me about how you have plans
to marry me
with an exact location in mind.
You'd call me your wife,
yet at the same time,
you'd tell me about these guys
who you would supposedly
envision your future with.

Everything had so much uncertainty.
Why do you think I never asked you the question?
You had me out here looking at rings
when we weren't even in a relationship.
How do you expect me
to get down on one knee
and ask you to be my one and only
when you couldn't even give me something
as simple as clarity.

It's okay, we weren't meant to be.

Sometimes the thought of your touch
becomes a little too much.
I've forgotten what it feels like
to have your hand intertwined with mine
when we would go on a drive,
or how the pronunciation of my name sounds
while rolling off of your tongue.

All of the memories of you, of us,
are washing away
like footprints in the sand,
and, as much as I want to pull you back
from getting sucked within the current, I can't.

# MANIC.

I'm hesitant
to hang up any of our framework
on the wall
and put it on display.

Why would I ever want to
g l o r i f y   t r a g e d y ,
and decorate pain
to promote something so negative
as if it deserves any type of space?

You never wanted me
to read any of your pages from the start,
but, you couldn't help it.

You let me read the ink
within your manuscript
despite your hesitation,
and, as soon as you did,
I became invested into the deepest parts
of your damaged heart
that you attempted to keep hidden.

I made sure to bookmark
every single scar and stretchmark
that you never dared to read out loud
from your table of contents,
no matter how traumatic.

I refuse to see you lose
a battle within your own self image
from topics that you've neglected to address.

# MANIC.

I don't know what it is
about pain,
but, she'll do anything to reach the surface
no matter how much of an inconvenience it is,
and somehow, she always manages to find a way
to be at the top of my priority list
of  b u r d e n s .

Just this once,
I don't want to be fixated
on having to give her attention,
but nonetheless,
she wears down my motivation,
constantly testing my patience
demanding to be addressed
and to feel noticed with recognition
the instant she becomes present.

I'M TORN
BETWEEN BEING AT WAR WITH PEACE
WITHIN MY OWN MENTALITY.
CONSTANTLY GOING BACK AND FORTH
AND QUESTIONING
IF I'M DESERVING
OF SUCH TRANQUILITY.

# MANIC.

I'm bleeding,
and it's because you're ripping me
a t   m y   s e a m s
that have yet to finish healing,
and now old problems are resurfacing.
How is any of this not causing you any worry,
do you not see what you're doing to me?

This is all your doing,
and now you have me wondering
if you even cared for my stitching
because you obviously
know how long it took me
to battle my depression, and anxieties.
They're leaking out faster than a current stream
and I'm the only one catching
as much as I can before they leave
as you're just standing over my shoulder,
watching me desperately on my knees.

She tells me,
*I feel so empty*
*I'm surprised that I haven't died*
*of alcohol poisoning.*
As she simultaneously
holds up the empty bottle of Jack in her hand
while making eye contact with me.

I couldn't decide
on which was more empty,
the whiskey glass or her eyes.

# MANIC.

Depression,
how would I describe it?

You make me colorblind.
I've lost sight
of the colors within the rainbow
because you decided to strip
every bit of it
and leave me with all of the blacks, greys and whites.
My sky is no longer vibrant
because you decided that it would be right
to make it achromatic and dull.

You make my bed
feel like I'm laying within a casket,
constantly suffocating,
gasping for air when it's already open.
Wondering if it's my time to leave for heaven
or fall into my descent
after my decision of wrapping the bondage
around my neck
and covering my wrists with bandages.

It's looking at a T.V. screen
and reading the headline
of another news story
about an underage human being
successfully dying by suicide and instantly becoming jealous
and questioning why it wasn't my time
when I had attempted. Twice.

It's a familiar, yet toxic friend
who you know you shouldn't associate yourself with,
but, you can't help it
because it has become a close shadow
that you've grown so comfortable to know.

# ANGELA SOLIS

And the thought of ever saying no
to the hands that have never let you go
by the throat
only feels like a sin.
How ironic.
I guess you just become accustomed
to the manipulative grip
and second guess your worth
because at the end of the day, you take it.

It's an unwanted attachment
that you can never admit to
because a double standard is in place
when the topic of mental illness becomes mentioned.
It's a battle of having to deal with the repercussions
of societies ignorant stigmas
stemmed from the media
creating an unrealistic
expectation to act as if you're undiagnosed,
or on any type of medication,
because in their eyes, *you're doing just fine.*
You're expected to not ruin the mood in the room
by deciding not to mention that you've had *thoughts of wanting to die,*
because speaking your truth,
that becomes *too selfish.*

Depression,
it's sitting within your own conscience
and contemplations in silence
at the dinner table, or 3AM at night
because everyone, including yourself,
has now deemed your own mental health a burden.

Depression,
it's a double ended blade
of debating on which one will cause me less pain.
*To leave or to stay?*

# MANIC.

I

don't

know

why

I still get ANXIOUS when I write.

I've never been one to sit back and be hesitant
to spread a message,
but, I guess
it's because of the type of topics
and the simple fact that my lines don't lie.
I'm left with constantly exposing
traumatic memories
that I would have never imagined sharing
in the name of healing.


I'm consistently conflicted.
It's making me continuously wonder
if anybody would ever be open minded
e n o u g h   t o   l i s t e n.
Leaving me to inevitably become distant
and left to sit
with the biggest question of concern,
am *I really being heard?*

# MANIC.

<u>Messages at 2AM</u>

"I LOVE YOU MAMA.
I'M SORRY FOR BEING ANYTHING
BAD TO YOU.
I TRY NOT TO BE
WHAT MY MOM AND DAD SHOWED ME
AND I HOPE ONE
DAY TO MAKE YOU PROUD THAT I'M YOUR MOM."


I watched you deteriorate
in the most painful way
physically and mentally
day by day,
and all I ever wanted to do
was to be able to take it all away.
It was never supposed to be this way.

I know you have your own unresolved problems
and issues,
but, I wanted you to want to work on us too.
I never liked hiding away
and staying in my bedroom,
but that's what I chose to do
because I refused
to have to see a version of you
that I know wasn't.

Do you know how long
I wanted you to just look at me
and feel seen?
Do you know how long
I craved for you to cry on my shoulder
and become the reason
why you would attempt to get clean
and sober?

I shouldn't have to be wondering

# ANGELA SOLIS

to myself at nine on why
you were spiraling
and questioning if any of it was because of me.


Look at me!


The alcohol and drugs
can't comfort you like me and the babies can
but you go back to it anyway.
That ethanol is your safe space, huh?
Who are you trying to runaway from?
Where are you trying to go?


Why is my sister calling me
in the middle of the night
while I simultaneously
get a drunk text from you apologizing?
And just like that, it clicks,
I know what's happening,
h i s t o r y   i s   r e p e a t i n g.


But all I can do as a big sister
is be there on a phone screen
asking her how she's feeling,
how she's coping with what you've made her see,
mentioning that I can pay for therapy
if she ever considers such a thing,
or letting her know that she can talk to me
because I know what it feels like to have to leave
out of a situation you put us in
and feeling guilty about not being
able to bring the others with me.


Why cant I be the reason you give it all up?
Shouldn't that,
shouldn't I,
shouldn't WE be enough?

# MANIC.

Her own flesh and blood
needs to be protected from her own self,
somebody call a Code 5150.

It makes me wonder
if this sickness, this mentality
is hereditary.

I've mentioned it to my therapist previously
by breaking down past experiences
eagerly questioning if such things
could ever be passed down to me.

*"Definitely,*
*there have been countless studies."*

My heart sank rapidly.
My mind started connecting everything,
string by string.
Making me unwillingly relive every
suicidal tendency
and traumatic memory,
scene by scene.

IT WAS ALL A FAÇADE.

OUR FOUNDATION
WAS NEVER BUILT ON LOVE.

IT WAS CONSTRUCTED
FROM THOUGHTS
ENCOMPASSED WITH LUST.

# MANIC.

When it came down to it,
I never understood your logic.

I always had to second guess
your thought process
because you could never settle on a decision
even when you were the one who would mention the topic.

You had me holding
onto the idea of a future like an ornament
when really, I was too blind to see
that you never had any intention
to invest in us.

In me.

I'm hesitant,
but sometimes I want to ask you the question
of where you think we disconnected?

Maybe it wasn't what I thought it was
to begin with
because you never knew
how to connect.
You were always notorious
with the way you would resist.

And if I'm being honest,
I think we bonded over trauma.
You only ever put effort
to contact me when something was wrong
so I can be your own personal dump
to take all your worries on your chest off.

# MANIC.

I DON'T RECOGNIZE MYSELF ANYMORE,
ALL I SEE IS AN OUTLINE
OF WHAT I USED TO BE
WITH AN UNHEALTHY IMBALANCE BETWEEN
LIGHT AND DARK SHADING.

AND ALL I'M LEFT WITH IS SELF REFLECTING
ON HOW I NEVER WANT TO BE THAT EMPTY
EVER AGAIN.

EVEN COMMITMENT
CAN BECOME LONELY.
IT'S BECOMING HEAVY.
MY FEET ARE CONSTANTLY DRAGGING
AND LOSING SENSE OF DIRECTION.

I'M LOSING ME.

MANIC.

I'M LOSING PIECES OF YOU ALTOGETHER,
AND I KNOW IT'S FOR THE BETTER.

ALL OF THE MEMORIES,
THESE PIECES, ARE NOW JUST A DISTANT MEMORY,
THAT I ONLY LOOK BACK ON OCCASIONALLY
TO HELP REMIND ME
THAT THEY WEREN'T MEANT TO BE
A PART OF ME PERMANENTLY.

ANGELA SOLIS

THE TIME I INVESTED IN YOU
IS TIME I CAN NEVER TAKE BACK,
AND EVEN THOUGH I DON'T REGRET
WHAT I THOUGHT WE HAD,
I WISH THAT I DIDN'T HAVE TO
COUNT ON MORE THAN ONE HAND
THE AMOUNT OF TIMES
I FELT LIKE YOU HAD
ALWAYS PUT ME LAST.

# MANIC.

Why are your decisions
always dipped in confusion?

Your mood swings
are worse than an ocean current
that has no sense of direction.

And your conscience.
It's empty
and malnourished
with nothing left to siphon.

Tragic.

You're so quiet and still,
but, I want you to know that I hear
and feel you more than usual tonight.

You make me emotional
with your presence being this heavy,

and I guess
that's why I choose to show my appreciation
in waves of spontaneity
and in every way that's reckless
as if it's my own love language
by feeling your breeze
graze over my body
as I lay down carelessly
on top of the roof of my Camry
holding onto nothing
but faith and empathy
while someone else is in control of the speed
beneath me
because for me, when there's unpredictability,
there comes peace
in my sanity.

# MANIC.

It's just us three
lost in the midnight summer breeze
with the audio from my Camry
roaring unapologetically.

But it really feels like two,
because it's in moments like these
that I wish I could remain oblivious
to the obvious
and I wasn't so aware of both your feelings
because as I watched both of your fingers
dance together all night
from the passenger side,
I couldn't help but wish that your hand
was entangled with mine.

# ANGELA SOLIS

It's scary
to finally realize
that the closer I had gotten to you,
the farther I had drifted away from me.

And now that I can see clearly,
I understand that I was clothed in a false reality.

Since the beginning
our personalities were rocky
with a foundation that wasn't built —
that wasn't meant to be kept sturdy
no matter how much I believed it to be
with an even more unpredictable platform.

I guess sometimes we need the heartbreak
to reach a happy ending
to start a new beginning.

# MANIC.

You killed
who you thought you were going to be a long time ago
because from your perspective
she was in critical condition.

As a matter of fact,
y o u   w e r e   t h e   o n e
who drew out the white body outline
with the chalk
and hid her behind
the yellow tape capitalized with

C A U T I O N.

We have a generation
that craves to be touched over every inch
of their body
that they forgot what it feels like to be nurtured
and cared for mentally
because they don't see intimacy
in any other way besides two bodies touching
instead of mental comforting.

A generation that acceded
to standards being so low
that no one even knows
what they want or desire
unless it's monetary,
put within arm's reach,
or if it's a late-night text
to Netflix & Chill,
for the opportunity to dig in a rib
and catch a lick
in attempt to have a connection
when they can't even remember
what the persons first name is.

No wonder love
is slowly becoming havoc.

At the end of the day
we've all bent over
and broken our own rules for somebody
whether it was intentional or not.

Sacrificing personal boundaries
became the normality
even if that meant pleasing
that somebody who could never see
the worth in your own being.

Your soul
becoming lost within a narcissistic ego
altered your moral compass,
disorienting your own sense of direction
and conscience.

Now,
you're left with a bruised

b

a

c

k

b

o

n

e

that's delicate and fragile
that shows
for what it's like
not being under your own control.

# MANIC.

*We're afraid to love,*
*but not afraid to crave lust.*


So, with that,
don't tell me about your thoughts,
no no, stop it,
that's too much to handle.


Just give me something physical
and easily accessible
like your hand.


Let me ignore and take advantage
of all the time that you make for me
and focus on all of your extremities
as an alternate.


Let me get distracted,
and crave
all of the things
that society has told me
I should put as a priority,
God forbid that you're a human being
with feelings.
By the way, didn't you hear?
We're not supposed to have those,
the moment we do
we're supposed to turn cold.

## ANGELA SOLIS

Why are you still warm?
I'm not here to blend temperatures
and have some sort of connection,
that makes me uncomfortable,
all I want is your most valuable asset,
time and attention.

But don't worry,
the moment
that my temporary satisfaction
is met, I'll ghost
even though I said I'm not like the rest.
So why are you hurt now?
We were never a thing.

 — You're afraid to love, and that's why you run.

# MANIC.

In the midst
of your state of numbness,
you put your hands over my skin
and trapped me within
the grip of your lips
when you know it's my bliss.

You're so insensitive,
you know that's one of my weaknesses,
yet, you still take advantage.

# TRIGGER WARNING:

### pg. 94 - 99

# MANIC.

I never thought I would write about this,
but I've convinced
myself enough to acknowledge
that it deserves a space
in my pages
just like every other topic.

So, If I'm being completely transparent,
some nights I still question
why it even happened
but all I know is,
I still blame myself
a n d   f e e l   t h a t   I   d e s e r v e d   i t.

Yet, I find it completely ironic,
because if this would have happened
to anyone else that I'm close with,
I would tell them the exact opposite.
That their bodies don't deserve to be treated
like a piece of meat
for someone else's advantage
in order to fulfill their selfish momentary satisfaction
despite the amount of alcohol in their system.

I don't know,
all I can say is is that I wasn't me
during this period of time.
Physically, I was just going through the motions,
mentally, I was deteriorating
and constantly engulfed in the numbness.
I refused to take any medication,
but I still acknowledged and accepted it
from the pharmacist
just so I could keep adding to my collection
for the sole purpose
of maintaining a backup plan
just in case I went through with another attempt.

# ANGELA SOLIS

In a multitude of ways,
I was careless
towards any of my decisions
that directly affected my health
because I didn't want any help.

I never really went to this bar to begin with,
but it's convenient,
it's literally right across the parking lot
in front of my apartment complex.
I had just gotten off of work, walked my dog,
and figured I would only be there for a brief minute,
so, I didn't even bother changing out of my uniform.

My stomach had been empty all day,
but to me, it was okay
because I wasn't hungry anyway,
I knew that in order for me to be able to keep drinking
I had to have at least something
in my tummy.
One meal and a couple drinks later,
you took a seat a couple rows away from me,
asking me for my name and having conversation.
It eventually led to me explaining
to you that I had not one bit of interest,
*"The only way that I would sleep*
*with you was if I were wasted,*
*and besides, I'd be thinking of someone else the whole time."*
Maybe it was harsh, but it was honest,
I figured you would get the hint,
I guess you didn't.

Fast forward a bit,
I had become a little tipsy,
shots were bought for me,
and I took them unapologetically.

# MANIC.

Now, you're closer to me,
you buy me a drink
even when I told you previously
that I'm grown, and that I could buy my own.
I had Jameson the whole night as I usually do
as my go to.
*"You drink tequila? Yeah? I bet you have to chase and make a face."*
*One shot of Tequila later,*
*IT'S BLACK.*

*All I know is,*
*I couldn't go back*
*and track anything after that for you*
*even if I wanted to.*

*Maybe it was egotistical of me,*
*but the moment that I heard I couldn't do something,*
*I had no hesitation with the liquid*
*touching my lips*
*when I subconsciously knew that I shouldn't.*

*IT'S BLACK.*

What's in my mouth?
I can't focus, everything is still blurry.
Where am I? Why am I turned around?
I can't feel anything, but I feel you.

It's 4am on a Friday work morning,
I don't know where my phone is,
*oh, there it is, it's dead.*
You finish, I pick
up all of my clothing
and head to my place to leave
without saying anything,
not remembering a single thing.

# ANGELA SOLIS

I put my shower on full heat
to give endless steam
making my vision get blurry
just like my memory.
I headed to work two hours early,
grabbed breakfast
received a heaven sent
negative HIV test
and had been injected with IV fluid
in order to help everything process
with proper nutrition and hydration
knowing I'm still not sober enough.
I sat alone in silence
knowing that I'm in denial
and I don't want to accept what just happened,
b u t   i t   d i d.

You find out my Instagram information
the next day to let me know
that I forgot a piece of clothing
at your place and you wanted to give it me.
I didn't care about it honestly,
all I cared enough for
was to retrieve
every lost puzzle piece
in my scatter-brained memory
even if was unfortunately one sided.

To keep it short,
I asked enough questions
to help with my sanity
and apparently
I made a move on you
before you dropped me off at my room.
According to you,
the next thing you knew
I went with you.

# MANIC.

I explained that the last thing
I could remember was being at the bar.
I don't remember walking home.
Being with you.
Being in your bedroom.
*I don't know what's true.*
All I know is
is this gut feeling
with a guilty conscious
saying that I shouldn't have put myself in that position.
But I don't know, it takes two to tango.


AM I CRAZY?
Why am I even second guessing
or questioning if what you did to me was okay
and that I deserved it.
Why am I not validating
my own emotions from this event?
I'm out here asking hypothetical questions
to my close friends that are men
and speaking to them in third person
asking if this is assault or even rape,
or if these words are being manipulative.
If my, if THIS, situation is even relevant.
Yet, here I am, doing just that,
how does that make any sense?!


I still feel dirty.
After all these months I still feel distant
from my own body.
I take full responsibility
for not acknowledging my surroundings,
but couldn't you see
that the alcohol had me disoriented?
I mentioned to you previously
that I was by no means interested.

# ANGELA SOLIS

You saw the opportunity
and you took advantage,
don't even try to deny it, because you did.
I still can't even describe how it was
because I was black out drunk
and numb.
All I see is fragmented images
and it's still not enough.
Maybe I should consider myself lucky
that I don't remember anything
because the thought of you on me
is still unsettling.
I don't even know your name,
but I still remember the way
that I couldn't feel you in between my legs.

I had every opportunity to leave,
I should have followed my intuition
and headed back to my apartment,
but I stayed anyways.

All it took was one poor decision,
that's all it took.
One shift could have made all the difference.

DO

YOU

UNDERSTAND

HOW HARD IT IS TO UNLEARN
THE NEEDS TO NURTURE
WOUNDS THAT YOU'VE GROWN SO CLOSE
TO KNOW

AS

IF

THEY

WERE

YOUR OWN?

I

DON'T

EXPECT

YOU

TO,

IT'S NOT SOMETHING I'D WANT

YOU

TO

GO

THROUGH

# MANIC.

I'm a mess
of unfinished thoughts,
sometimes they have nowhere to settle
because I struggle at explaining
certain emotions.

It's to the point
where I failed at giving them the proper attention
without building a stable enough foundation
to have a concrete destination
to bring proper fruition
to help release every single outlet.
So, I developed the habit
of planting them in every place
beside the position it was intended.

My mirror reflection
becomes nonexistent
after a couple seconds.

Sometimes the words become overly stretched
that I can't even read the message
due to the distortion.

The voices become too hectic
and the skin becomes delicate
after a certain amount of slashes.

# MANIC.

Baby,
this doesn't have to be your fate.
You can change,
you hear me?
You deserve to have a place
within your mental space
that's comfortable and safe
enough to make you want to stay.

Don't stay
where you are constantly
left with wanting to run away,
you're allowed to change the pace.
You need to part ways
with this feeling of astray,
it doesn't deserve to be entertained.

You're completely drained,
what point are you trying to make?
I'm well aware of all of your damage
and how much you can take,
but just because you're used to the pain
doesn't mean it should be sustained.

You don't have to repeatedly break
in order to prove that you have the ability
to mend.

The parts of your inner being
that have yearned to be seen
in between the seams
became bleak.

Mental stimulation
became non-existent
way too often.

Sexual healing,
manifested into physical dissociation
more than I'd like to admit.

And sexual tension
grew into a distraction
in order to avoid having to connect
with emotions
that have been forgotten
due to the lack on contact.

— Dissatisfaction is the price of dissociation.

# MANIC.

You're numb.

You're drinking away aimlessly
as if you'll find the answers to all of your problems
at the bottom
of that glass bottle
even if that means
losing sensation in your tongue.

There's no answers
down there, love,
just empty feelings, I promise.

I find myself reminiscing
and relapsing
over my old laugh.

I miss the one I used to have.

Because ever since she left me
I haven't had the chance
to go back
and hold her within my grasp.

# II : MARK

# II:CORINTHIANS

# MANIC.

HER HAIR REMINDED
ME OF FIRE,
AND I WASN'T AFRAID OF GETTING BURNED.

# ANGELA SOLIS

There's only two percent
of her kind in the world population,
and to be honest,
her presence
deserves more appreciation.
Whether it be from giving praise
to her growth in becoming more outspoken
because she used to be timid,
or from leaving her previous
abusive relationships,
she deserves all of the recognition.
And I'm pretty sure the sun notices
it because it hits different
as soon as it glistens
off of her hair,
reminding me of my favorite red wine
even though she prefers white,
Rosatello Moscato,
if we are getting specific.

—

And her eyes,
they change depending on her outfit
or mood,
because they go from green, to grey, to blue
in an instant,
and it's so hard for me to choose
which ones to get lost in
when I just want to pause time for a second
and appreciate every stage
that they go in
before they transition.

# MANIC.

How could you possibly
expect me
to go to an art exhibit
and stare at all of these pieces
mounted all over the walls
when all I do is become distracted
from the true masterpiece
t h a t   i s   y o u ,
who is right in front me
when I can see every
detail in you that is empty
that's meant to be
filled in by me.

HER WORDS ARE LIKE STICKERS
AND I WANT THEM ALL OVER ME.

# MANIC.

I carry pain and trauma
within my mind and body,
and I travel with her often.
I pack her away in my backpack
until we land
to our next destination
to show her that there's still so much more to see,
that there's still so much more air to breathe,
and reasons to keep fighting
because there is no timeline to healing.
I hold her weight on my shoulders
no matter how much it hurts
b e c a u s e   I   n e e d   h e r   t o   s e e
it's all for adventures like this,
places we have yet to plant our feet,
people we have yet to meet,
and words we have yet to spread
for others to read.

Will you ever let me shower you
with all of my attention?
I know you're hesitant
to accept it
because you've given
me an abundant
amount of resistance,
but I feel like I've proven
my devotion.
And if I'm being honest,
I deserve reciprocation.
I no longer want to hide
the depths of my love
by keeping my feelings unattended
like this anymore
when I just want to explore
every inch
of my own warmth.

# MANIC.

I learned about street poetry
because of her,
and although I'm still understanding
how the whole thing
works,
I'm at least learning
the way her mind wanders,
and how her heart sinks
into someone her mind
c o u l d   n e v e r   r e l e a s e
from feeling everything ocean deep.

Do you even think about me?
Apparently
you talk about me in therapy,
but you haven't bothered responding
to any
of my missed calls or messages
because you're subconsciously pushing
me farther away by the day,
and there's nothing I can do or say
about it besides accepting
the fact
that I have to just sit back
and understand
that I have to let the cards unfold
how they are meant to be
rather than trying
to force my selfish needs
of keeping you close to me.

# MANIC.

You told me
you'd never leave.
You're pushing me away
by self-sabotaging
everything and I don't know
how to feel besides being
i n  d i s b e l i e f
because I truly believed
that this would never happen;
At least not to you and me.
I'm trying to not take this personally
and give you all the space you need,
but, I'd be lying
if I said that I was fine
with the whole situation
because I'm checking out mentally,
and that's what's scary.
I don't want to leave,
I really don't,
but if this is a sign
for me to tend to my own growth,
then that's what I'll follow.

LET ME INTO YOUR HEADSPACE
FOR JUST A MINUTE.
I WANT TO DECODE YOUR SUBCONSCIOUS
AND TURN YOUR THOUGHTS INTO POETRY.

# MANIC.

Baby girl,
What are you so scared of?
Commitment?
I know it's a hard question
to answer,
and an even harder decision
to go through with,
but one day,
you'll have to make the decision
and just allow every emotion in
without the fear of negative repercussions
and the continuous, "What ifs?"
I wish I could be selfish
with you and show you what an honest
relationship is and have you all to myself,
but love isn't rushed.
It wouldn't be fair to you
and most importantly,
it wouldn't be fair to me.
We both deserve our own mental growth,
we deserve love that's monogamous,
and we both deserve love that feels like home.

# ANGELA SOLIS

I don't blame you
for feeling the way that do you.
If I didn't have to compartmentalize
the amount of emotional volume
I'm capable of
and were able to feel everything at the intensity
that I do,
I'd fall apart too.

# MANIC.

*AT THE END OF THE DAY,
YOU'RE THE RISK I'LL ALWAYS TAKE.*

Can I just love you outside
of every line
that you never dared to trace over?

I know you're comfortable
with choosing to play it safe,
but, I, on the other hand,
make impulsive and audacious decisions
because I don't love with training wheels,
and I have all of the scabs, scars and bruises
to prove it.

So, I know that it may sound foreign
and out of the ordinary
for you to be told to stop thinking
for a minute.
To embrace every scrape and cut
and follow your gut,
but, where would the fun
in falling in love
be if you didn't *love recklessly?*

# MANIC.

I want you
to hold me
just as tightly
as every string
on my ripped denim jeans.

For you
to trace your fingertips
over every inch
of my anatomy
as you study my curves
and learn
every foreign detail over my skin.

For you
to reach out
with your desperate
hands that are so eager
to strip every layer of clothe
on my body off.

For you
to consciously leave
your signature
stains of permanent ink
imprinted all over me.

Unapologetically.

Her curves are my favorite
piece of poetry
to seep through me
because she writes and reads
the pages
of my body effortlessly.

She's my favorite script
to strip
down word by word,
line by line.

Leaving me on my knees,
desperately
waiting to be
engulfed by the serenading
notes of her moans
sending chills through my bones.

# MANIC.

I HOPE YOU KNOW
THAT FOREPLAY
STARTS WAY BEFORE YOU
EVEN TOUCH HER.

# ANGELA SOLIS

The image
of your silhouette
has been imprinted
in every inch of my memory
and I can't fathom the thought
if it vanishing.

I'm not interested
in having just a peak
of your carving,
I'm invested
in your whole being.
I want to divulge
deeper than what's on your surface
and indulge
in every detail of you that you keep
distant and private.

So, let me strip
you of every bit
of your depiction
until there's nothing left
except your bare submission.

I want you to be permanent.

# MANIC.

Just this once,
can we just
fall in love
without having to constantly
worry about how hard our impact will be
and embrace the landing?

I'm ready.

# ANGELA SOLIS

Baby girl,
take that cigarette
out your mouth
and let me be
the one who takes away the breath
from your chest.

# MANIC.

YOU SUBDUE MY NERVES
AND STIR
ME NERVOUS.

HOW IRONIC.

I'm a
sucker
for a
pretty
view.

So, I've been
stuck
looking at
you.

MANIC.

You're picking off
all of my petals
from my branch,
but you remembered the thorns
so, you didn't mind your hand
becoming poked and stabbed
b e c a u s e   y o u   k n e w
that even the most beautiful
things in this world
are hard to grasp.

I have so much substance,
it is inevitable
for me to get lost
in the depth
of my own essence.

# MANIC.

If you're comfortable enough,
may I practice
the silent language
of Braille
all over your masterpiece
until I eventually
become fluent
of your embodiment?

I pinky promise,
you don't have to say a word,
because I've been studying
every layer of your smooth texture
of a home,
including the parts
that you are
the most self-conscious with
that have become forsaken
and don't get the proper attention,
like the scar under your chin
that you got from when you were a kid,
or your lines
that spread vertically along your thighs
like tiger stripes
with stretch marks that extend
across your hips
more than you're comfortable for others to witness.

Just sit back, relax,
and let me be attentive
to every little bit
of you that's been neglected
from my absence.

It's you,
I want you to stay.
And the best way
that I can do such a thing
is write about you on a page
even if it never mentions your name,
because then at least
t h i s   w a y ,
you do stay.

MANIC.

STOP
BEING
SO
DAMN
INTIMIDATED

WITH CONNECTION,
LOOK INTO ME FOR A MINUTE.

How does it feel
to have a tangible
paperback of my love
in your hands
encompassing
only half of my intensity?

Imagine
if
you
had
the
whole
thing?

# MANIC.

Tell me,
why is there always
so much honesty
from the sound of one's voice
at 3 in the morning?

Everything is still,
except the conversations,
the topics
become more intense; candid.

You're such a work of art,
and it's so hard
for me not to stare;
You're a rarity.

And what blows me away,
is you can't even see yourself in that way.

But, that's okay,
because at the end of the day,
I get to appreciate
and swoon
over you in a multitude of ways.

I just hope and pray
that you will eventually change
your perspective of yourself
and come to see the value of your growth
from every phase.

IF ONLY YOU COULD COMPREHEND
HOW THERAPEUTIC
EACH AND EVERY
ONE OF YOUR VERSES BECOME
ONCE YOU FILL UP
A PAPER SHEET
WITH LIMITLESS FEELINGS;
UNFILTERED AND UNAPOLOGETICALLY.

# ANGELA SOLIS

If you have time tonight,
would you mind
dancing with my waves
under the moonlight,
and getting lost in my lullaby?

I want to pull you into me,
like gravity,
and have you get lost in my tide.

I give you permission
to set foot into my ocean,
a n d  t o  f a l l  d e e p e r
than what I show on the surface
without you having to worry
about an aggressive current
despite my reputation,
because with you,
I'll be cognizant
enough to be delicate.

So, as I open up my emotions
and allow you to walk into the depths
of my ocean,
just promise
me that you won't take advantage.

# MANIC.

If there's one thing that I can guarantee
to you,
it's that anything worth having
is going to leave you a little dirty.

Having you dripped in experience,
covered in residue,
and making others who ever encounter you
wonder what you've gone through.

But, oddly enough,
I'm fine with things
turning out a bit messy,
because being clean is the last thing
that I ever want it to be
if that means
it'll stop me from growing.

WRAP
ME
UP
IN YOUR LOVE LANGUAGE.

AND
DRENCH
ME
IN YOUR ESSENCE.

# MANIC.

We haven't spoken in a month
because I cut you off,

but today, you messaged me
Happy Birthday
and that you *love and miss me.*

I thanked you and said I love you too
but this time, it wasn't how it used to be,
it was platonically,
and that's what made all the difference to me.

I'm healing.

I'm not in tune with this half-ass type of love,
I'm not sure about you, but,
I could never relate
because it's just not in my DNA.
Loving hard, and passionately is in my blood,
it just comes to me naturally.

So, I don't understand your confusion,
have you never experienced a love so selfless?
I need you to realize that the things
you are asking for are not tedious,
they should be expected,
and never pushed to the side or neglected,
so, don't worry
because when it comes to me
you don't have to ask for any of this,
it's included in my package.

# MANIC.

I mean it, I promise.

This will be the last time
that I deny
addressing every type
of feeling that I've been holding onto inside
b e c a u s e   o f   m y   p r i d e .

This will be the last time
that I shove my insecurities and sensitivities
to the side lines,
and treating them as if they're undeserving
of being given just as much attention and light.

I'm madly
in love with all the details.

They're so subtle, yet intricate.
Personal, yet delicate.

It's intimate,
and to be able to know any of your complexities is a gift.
The messages within
your being are hidden within the obvious
and I intend on learning as much of your fine lines
that I can manage,
it just depends on how I handle it.

# MANIC.

If you were to ask me
where my mind has been wandering,

I'd tell you
that I've been thinking
about how much I value you,
and that as long as I have you next to me,
then there's nowhere else I'd rather be.

I couldn't resist keeping
this type of scenery
all to myself.

I wanted to share the beauty
and submerge you in the evergreen
w i t h   m e .

So, naturally,
that's what I did,
because what would the point in all of this be
if I chose to be selfish
and decided to only allow my eyes to witness
such imagery
when I now have the opportunity
to turn a memory
that was once mine, to now be
between you and me.

# MANIC.

Show me where no one ever goes,
I want to get lost
in that mind of yours
of a rabbit hole
and become enchanted
with all of your madness.

I don't understand why others are intimidated
by what makes you different.

UNWRAP ME
LIKE YOUR FAVORITE PIECE
OF CANDY.

I PROMISE YOU I'M SWEET.

MANIC.

I JUST WANT TO INGEST YOU IN
AND TAKE IN ALL OF YOUR NUTRIENTS
FOR MY OWN BENEFIT

NO MATTER HOW SELFISH
THAT IS AS A DECISION.

# ANGELA SOLIS

When I really think about it,
poets are always split
between being a little bit
b r o k e n   a n d   s e l f i s h .

So, I guess you can go ahead
and call me a little selfish
because my words are never intended
to reach the masses.
Outsider eyes were never meant
to read my own hidden messages
because they have never been the true target.

The true intentions
are solely for my own benefit
so I can finally listen and pay attention
to the problems that I have left neglected.

# MANIC.

I'VE SEEN
A LOT OF THINGS,
BUT I'VE NEVER SEEN MY SPIRIT
GLOW AS BRIGHTLY
AS IT'S BEEN
WHEN IT'S WITH YOU.

TO BE
AN ARTIST
IS TO UNDERSTAND THAT THIS
GIFT YOU HAVE BEEN GIVEN
IS NOW A UNIQUE
LOVE LANGUAGE.

# MANIC.

I'm in awe
of you after all.

I ache to get lost
in every high and fault
within your dialogue.

I'm not used
to scratching the surface
when I intend on reaching depth
as my final destination.

So, just know that it'll be nothing new
t o   m e ,
but everything foreign to you
when I decide to undo
every hidden layer of your being.

# ANGELA SOLIS

Let me give you images that last.
I know you're used to distortion
with faded colors
and burnt edges,
but, with me,
I pinky promise you
that I can give you enough pigment
within every inch
of your portraits
that you'll finally want to frame it.

# MANIC.

"How many?"
is the real question for me.

How many
more days do I get
to be blessed with your presence?

How many
more days do I get
to have the opportunity to invest
in every aspect
of you?

How many more sunrises
get to bless our eyes
and how many more sunsets
do we get to lose our breath
over before we reach an end?

-

Honestly, I'm not sure,
and quite frankly,
that's too many questions
to try to control or worry about
when I can soak it all in
and enjoy every single second instead.

That's the things about being an artist,
it's being blessed
with the possession
of having our own unique love language
with there being a multitude of options
for us to get lost in a process
from a new project
while simultaneously spreading a message,
whether it be from words
being typed to be read,
or putting poetry in motion
with a paintbrush and acrylics.

THE DEVIL HAS BEEN REAL QUIET LATELY.
I HAVENT HEARD HIS VOICE OF TEMPTATION
TO LEAVE
OR DO ANYTHING NEGATIVE PHYSICALLY.
I THINK
HE SEES THAT I FINALLY HAVE GOD NEXT TO ME.

# ANGELA SOLIS

I've refrained from writing
about you for quite some time now
because I have no filter.

And the thing is,
I can't lie,
so, I'm not sure where my lines
would take me when I willingly decide
to allow you to be
the main topic.

But, like I said,
I'm unsure
on how to allow myself to write about her
because all I know is the words
would be too pure
to be heard.

# MANIC.

It's a *different type of scenery* isn't it?

To lay down on the empty
movie theatre parking lot concrete
without a single care or worry
during the summer heat
in the middle of the evening.

And even though I couldn't guarantee
that we would perceive the same thing,
we  would  at  least  see
the same lightening
on one side, and simultaneously speak
of the fine purple and pink sky line
with a lifespan that doesn't have enough time
before it would vanish into the night.

I just wanted us to get lost in the evening
sky for a second
and to stare deeply in what we couldn't see,
because sometimes the loudest things
are what we blindly overlook,
yet, ironically
I failed to realize that I got lost in you
during the process.

## ANGELA SOLIS

Sometimes people just can't let go of the past,
and damn,
it makes me wonder to myself
if you ever lost view of your path.

People expect you to hold
onto the things
that you hold onto dearly
even if your knuckles start to bleed,
even if you're suffering
because they don't see
that the very thing
that you thought you could never leave
needs to be.

Those people that control your strings
don't have an ounce of worry
about your well being
because as long as they're leeching
and benefiting
off of what you're doing,
then they'll stand next to you proudly
until that's you who's in need
of someone to strengthen your knees.

But little do they know,
you've been working on yourself silently,
g r o w i n g   g r a d u a l l y .
And you're going to get where you want to be
because you will no longer be a slave
to the past memories.

# MANIC.

I created
an environment
within myself
that rooted off of malnourishment
towards any positive affirmations.
I've felt neglected
for so long
that I forgot what it felt
like to be wanted.

I created a space
that pushed away
any type of love that came my way,
and all that ever left me with was to question
anyone who ever wanted me
in their association
and walked with me in the same direction
when I didn't even want to be within
my own presence.

I guess
I can just come to the conclusion
t h a t   t h e r e ' s   m o r e   t o   m e
that what I think is only on the surface.

    — I'm not worthless as I believed myself to be.

All you ever do now is experience
copious amounts of suffocation
from the abundant
amount of love deprivation
resulting from your own self abandonment
because you chose to remain negligent
towards what you were supposed to address.

And in that process,

you forgot the definition
of true connection.

You conformed to becoming addicted
to dissociation
that you succumbed to the numbness
because you came up
with the distorted notion
that in order to feel anything
meant to also embody "weakness"
and that's the very thing you've tried to deflect.

I guess
no one told you that there's strength
in having a cognizant relationship
with your own emotions.

# MANIC.

I know a masterpiece
when I see one,
so, when I saw you,
my first instinct
was to instantly
enclose you in a picture frame
and put you on display
so everyone can appreciate
you the same way.

But, then it hit me,
and I came to the realization that women –
women like you,
don't deserve to be stuffed within
a box of limited inches
that would evidently keep your growth restricted.

You're limitless,
you should be treated like it.

I'm usually not one
to become tongue tied,
but she just holds something
that's difficult to describe.

She's easy on the eyes,
and light on my mind,
pulling me into her center like gravity,
so serene.

Nothing is ever heavy,
there's no weight,
and no pressure.

This is healthy.

# MANIC.

I need you to love what you have
before what you love becomes
something of the past
and you're forced to be left with
w h a t  y o u  h a d
because you didn't appreciate
it enough when you had the chance.

They will say anything
under the sun,
but I will do everything
under the moon.

Actions speak louder than words.

– For M.K.N

# MANIC.

Promise me
everything that you could never keep.

Tease me
with all of your manipulative sweet nothings.
Show me
more of your bittersweet
i n c o n s i s t e n c i e s,
and flood every cavity
within my lungs
full of your diluted attention.

Because with that, I'll walk away at ease
knowing that this is what love will never be,
and everything
that will forever emulate toxicity.

The voice of your eyes
is deeper
than any language
ever created.

Let me interpret
your every message
o n e   s e n t e n c e
at a time.

— Just for you, I will become fluent.

YOUR MIND BECAME
MY FAVORITE PLACE
TO ESCAPE.

YOUR PRESENCE
BECAME MY SAFE SPACE.

# ANGELA SOLIS

You.

Let me confess about you
a little while longer.

Allow me to describe you in such a way
that everything about you are take a ways,
like how your eyes
are meant to be
written down and described by authors like me
with retrieved memories
who save more than just a page
in order to give you the vision of you that I see.

But most importantly,
to be given the accessibility
to the complexity of your mind
that artists only dream
of being able to have such opportunity
to dissect
in their lifetime.

# MANIC.

I think about you often
and the way you've impacted me.
Your presence
nurtures my anxieties.

You unapologetically
wrap around my ears
with your free-flowing melodies—
a never-ending serenade just for me.

The way your body
kisses the sun as it's setting
in the evening
never ceases to amaze me,
you don't even realize your own impact
from your reflection glistening.

The sand between my feet
becomes grounding,
the touch of your hand
is cradling.

Since the beginning,
your free-flowing personality
rubbed off on me,
and the moment
I became old enough to become
m e s m e r i z e d   a n d   t e r r i f i e d
of your own depth
at the exact same time
that's when I knew
that I wanted to be just as impactful as you.

— The ocean is calling me.

What grounds you?

What grounds me?

The oceans wave and currencies,
she always has a pull on me.

The mountain trails and it's evergreen trees,
they help me breath.

The Earth's heartbeat, really.

# MANIC.

Can we drive around
until we get lost
with both our palms
and fingers intertwined
while looking at the skyline
as if you were mine?

# ANGELA SOLIS

I don't know who needs to hear this
because deep down, I wish
my younger self did.

But, one day,
you will eventually learn how to love the sound
of your own footsteps
walking away from the things
that are no longer meant for you.

# MANIC.

You should tell
the one who you love and care for
that you love them.
Whether it's a friendship,
relationship,
platonic,
or romantic.

You should tell them, right?

Maybe I should take my own advice.

You say often
that *eyes are the window to the soul.*


Or how you want to play with *strings*
like Geppetto
and how you'll pick off all the *petals*
from every single rose
in the meadow
despite the amount of thorns shown.


I guess
my questions to you is,
can you see through me
like transparency?


Do you enjoy the view
of what has bloomed
and being able to see
that the previous roots have become lifeless,
with branches now limp?


— Progress.

# MANIC.

She has so many colors on her,
and I have so many blank spaces
to be filled.

I want to be selfish
and strip
as many as I can
into my hands.

Maybe,
I could be her empty canvas instead
because then,
she would spread
all of her colors on me
that I've been longing for
so desperately.

      − I want her to add to me.

I'm not sure
what I want to be,
but, maybe,
I can start off with being
your summer heat
that glazes over your body.
Or become your favorite pile of leaves
that you jump into every
fall season.
The snow that touches your tongue
and ocean that engulfs your feet.

I don't want or need
to be your everything.

Maybe I can just be
some of your most heartfelt memories.

# MANIC.

You deserve a perspective
that isn't limited.
So, if you let me,
I'll show you a life
that forces you to
look through a different type of lens
and question every decision
you have ever had before this.

One that has no set
of sense of direction
for a particular destination,
but, to a place
that is a safe space for a mind to rest.

One so full of adrenaline
that it lacks hesitation,
and the fear of being reckless
becomes nonexistent.
You'll eventually become addicted
to the feeling of unrestricted existence.

A life
that's no longer concerned with risks
or filled with all the what ifs,
but engulfed in an endless curiosity
of everyday living
where childhood dreams
and missed opportunities meet.

So, come have a leap of faith with me,
let's both be unapologetically carefree.

At the end of the day,
I think one of the hardest things
will always be
to reveal
the intensity of everything that you feel
when you originally intended
on keeping it sealed.

TELL
HER
HOW
YOU
FEEL.

# MANIC.

Do you notice the little things?
Like every single hidden message
in between my honest statements.

I leave context clues
just for you
and sometimes I wonder
if you ever resonate with each symbol
that I methodically choose
because the organization
is all for your eyes to attend to.

I know that I never say a name directly,
but I think I give off enough of you.

Maybe you're oblivious
and it goes right over your head,
either way,
I just want to know if you write about me too.
Or when I write a love poem
and you enjoy it,
does it remind you of somebody else
when it's actually about yourself?

I know I can't make songs for you
to blast on your stereo
that describes the way I feel for you
in a harmonic tune
like others can

# ANGELA SOLIS

but I guess this pen and notepad
will have to do
at the moment,
but, I'll take what I can,
because as long as you're able to hear me
when you read
the words that are on this page,
then I think I'll be okay.

I just want to know,
do you think of somebody else
in these words
that were written for you?

# MANIC.

## Self-Love

There's no need to rush,
I want us,
I want you,
to take your time with this type of love.

I know you're used to
being on the run
without taking any pit stops,
but, with me, I'll make you want to pause.

So, during your break
let me nourish you
and all of the tarnished roots
that you've forgot to tend to.

Don't be embarrassed of your damage, honey,
let me show you consistency
in every type of avenue
with words that have value
from matching my actions
that are a direct reflection
of my love language.

You're delicate,
I get it,
but I can handle it.
I'm not intimidated
by what makes you sensitive.
I'm invested,
so let me hear your emotions
and validate every single one of them.

# ANGELA SOLIS

You can call it selfish,
but I'm attracted
to the rawness
of allowing yourself to be seen,
I know it's not easy.

You're not a burden,
let me pay attention
to every section
of you that has been neglected,
every single word
from your sentences
that were never noticed
when all you've ever wanted was to be heard.
Every part of you that has become hardened
can become softened
with my tenderness.

Come inside for a minute,
you deserve to be appreciated,
I won't let you get lost again,
I promise.

MANIC.

I'M ENTIRELY AND COMPLETELY UNAPOLOGETIC
ABOUT WHO I CHOOSE TO KISS
BECAUSE I WANT

E
V
E
R
Y

B
I
T

OF HER MINDSET AND SURFACE.

SO, IF LOVING YOU IS A SIN,
SO BE IT,
I WANT ALL OF IT —

ANGELA SOLIS

E
V
E
R
Y

S
I
N
G
L
E

I
N
C
H

# MANIC.

They say that in the end,
everything in life is temporary.

Situations.

Relationships.

Mindsets.

Feelings.

People that we once knew.

But, what about you?
I can never have you be in the category
of being temporary.
You're too special of an individual
to me to ever be
just a transient memory
who would later be
explained in past tense
within a story.

You're here to stay with me.

ANGELA SOLIS

(A HAIKU FOR YOU)

TELL ME YOU LOVE ME,

I WILL GIVE YOU ALL OF ME

UNTIL THE EARTH STOPS.

Twin Flames
*(I'll tell you about her)*

I want to tell you about you.
But this time I won't have the taste
of wine on my lips,
and I promise you everything that I said, I meant it.
I hope that I can do you justice by this poem, but just know
that this still doesn't describe
the way that you make me feel.

*What's a soul mate?*
*For me? It's you.*

There's nothing about me that you don't know,
there's nothing about me
that I wouldn't want you to not know,
because there's something
about you that allows my vulnerability
to hit its peak, even when I subconsciously
want to hide away every single feeling.
But I just can't.

Because of you,
*you make me grateful that I'm here,*
and I don't even know why I'm crying
as I'm typing, or as I'm reading,
but all I know is, is that I'm happy,
and I'm happy that it's you.

*You make fear nonexistent.*
*You make risk feel like a benefit.*
*You make vulnerability feel precious.*
*You make this life better knowing that you're in it.*

I wish I could tell you how many days and nights
that I've prayed for a soul like you to come into my life.
For it to *come out the blue and flow like the sea,*
*so naturally.*
*You and me.*

You make me see that my baggage isn't heavy
and even if it is in that moment
you believe in me enough to keep going.

174

# ANGELA SOLIS

*You don't give me purpose,*
*you remind me that I have one,*
*you don't hold my heart in your hands*
*you merely put yours over mine*
*holding onto me tight, you add.*
*You're not my breath,*
*but you guide me to find my own oxygen.*

*You make feeling easy.*

*You make me, my sensitivities,*
*my heartbeat, feel seen,*
*just like on the way to the beach,*
*where I didn't have to fear or worry*
*about anything leaving.*

The countless memories that we've shared make me see
that I was supposed to keep breathing,
because all of this,
I wouldn't have wanted to miss one bit of it.

I catch myself remembering
when I was on the floor
merely lifeless from an overdose
and now, fast forward,
I'm on the floor dying of laughter.

And I'm cognizant
enough to know that I'm usually hesitant
on the future and promises
but with you, I'm confident.
With you I'm safe in every way.
Whether you see it or not,
you make me better in every aspect,
and I'm forever grateful.
I'm forever thankful for this type of love,
and this type of trust
because there will never be another you.

*So, what's a soulmate in my eyes?*
*It's you. You're mine.*

# MANIC.

"YOU ENHANCE ME IN EVERYTHING,
AND I GROUND YOU,
I HELP YOU THINK THINGS THROUGH."

## ANGELA SOLIS

For a minute,
can we role play as if
you were mine?

I want my lips
to kiss your mind
and have every bit
of your desires
spread all over me.

I want your legs
to spread and release
all of your fears and anxieties
with ease
as your hands
grip my back unapologetically
even if that means
my skin starts to bleed
just so your baggage
can become less heavy.

I want your heart
along with every scar
to be stripped
completely naked
and our energies
to connect
skin to skin.

Let me please
and love every
part of your being.

# MANIC.

Nobody ever catches my eye
long enough to hold it
if I'm being honest.

I fall for *intricate minds*
and *deep soulful eyes,*
so, when it came to you
you caught me by surprise.

You still do, every time.

ANGELA SOLIS

WHAT YOU WOULD DO FOR ME
I'D DO FOR YOU.

TIMES TWO.

# MANIC.

I JUST NEED YOU TO KNOW,
BY NO MEANS ARE YOU THE REASON
WHY I CHOOSE TO LIVE,
BUT WITHOUT A DOUBT

YOU REMIND ME WHY IT'S SO BEAUTIFUL TO DO SO.

I don't want or need the things
that others can
easily gain accessibility to.

I  fall
for the *priceless* things.

Like *hands dancing*
once they become intertwined,
or *honest eyes*
when they become locked with mine.

LET ALL THAT YOU DO
BE DONE IN LOVE.

1 CORINTHIANS 16:14

## DEAR READER,

Thank you from the bottom of my heart for being open enough to read my words.
And of course, I have to thank God for gifting me with the ability to write okay enough
make others feel something.

Here's my second book, MANIC.
She came out of know where, yet at the perfect time and I couldn't be more proud.
There's so much self reflection, growth, awareness and maturity in this book that it makes
emotional. I think a huge part of that is just me being completely cognizant towards my 1
of nurturing to my childhood self, you know? This book is me tending to years of old wo
being transparent with what I'm feeling instead of distracting myself and finally being willi
address my own emotions and feelings.
Little Ang had always wanted this - to just feel loved enough by myself, and to be underste
such a way that felt validated, and not from others, but again, just from herself and God.

So, writing this book and learning more about myself as a young woman has really given m
childhood self all the validation I was praying for. I finally feel heard by my own self,
everything is clear and less scrambled. But most importantly, I'm healing, it's definitely no
linear and self discovery is not easy, but this book shows the healing process from the past
present and it's in your damn hands.

But you know, at the end of the day I just want to create.
Whether it's drawing, painting, writing, whatever the hell it is that my heart guides me to,
I plan to keep creating whatever that is.

So, moving onto writing with what's on my heart, that's what this book is, I left it all then
my pages are where my heart is, it's my mind. I know what I've been blessed with and I'm
grateful that I have the tools, people and resources to share this type of art and creativity
without any filter or feeling as if I'm limited with restrictions.

Creativity and art isn't designed to have restrictions,
you're here to create whatever your heart pours out.

ssage to all of my creatives – know that your art is worth more than anyone else's
ons. Invest in yourself and in your own craft until you can't anymore.

't really believe in things being wasted because everything happens for a reason,
' my two attempts would have been successful, then these two books wouldn't exist,
two less things in this world.
God said to stay, you're not done, keep creating.

n telling you, whatever it is, whatever you're passionate about, please pursue it, pass it
HARE it. Stop thinking so much, let it come naturally, that's part of being a creator,
times things don't always come to you and you have to understand that that is simply part
e journey and being an artist.

e appreciate the process of things. Don't get too wrapped up with the final result, and
mber why you started. You never know what it can do for other people as well as yourself.

reate beautiful things unapologetically. This world needs it.

- FOREVER GRATEFUL,

Ang xoxo

# ANGELA

PHOTO BY ANDY RENTERIA

# SOLIS

ARTWORK BY J. SOLIS

# MANIC.

CPSIA information can be obtained
at www.ICGtesting.com
Printed in the USA
LVHW020934300321
682936LV00027B/894